SIGHT WORD BRACELETS
by
Dwayne Douglas Kohn

The copying, transmission or unauthorized reuse of this work not only violates federal copyright laws, punishable by civil and criminal sanctions, but is also highly unethical. Reproduction of these materials is permitted for classroom use by the purchaser only. Reproduction of these materials for an entire school or school district is strictly prohibited.

Smart As A Fox Teaching Materials are available from your local teacher supply store or purchase online at: www.MisterKindergarten.com. For materials in Spanish, please visit: www.PrimerGrado.com. We publish over 100 titles in a variety of languages.

SMART AS A FOX
BOX 4334
OCEANSIDE, CALIFORNIA
92052-4334

©2015 Smart As A Fox

SIGHT WORD BRACELETS

A student who has mastered 100 of the most common words in the English language is on his/her way to becoming a fluent reader! These 100 words form the basis of reading. You will be amazed how many of these words appear in the text of a typical newspaper article or on a random page of a book.

Children will LOVE learning sight words with these bracelets! Each time they make a new bracelet, your students will race home to share their new word with their family!

HOW TO MAKE

Note that the words are presented in the Rainbow Word order in the front of the book, followed by the words in alphabetical order. To make the bracelets, simply color the word and picture, cut out rectangle and staple ends together to create a sight word bracelet you can actually wear!

You may make the bracelet fit tiny wrists by pinching the excess bracelet together and using a piece of tape to make it a better fit. Make it just big enough so that the child is able to slip the bracelet on and off without tearing it.

100 WORDS

The 100 sight words in this title are:

a, about, after, all, an, and, are, as, at, be, been, but, by, call, can, come, could, day, did, do, down, each, find, first, for, from, get, go, had, has, have, he, her, him, his, how, I, if, in, into, is, it, its, just, know, like, little, long, look, made, make, many, may, more, most, my, no, not, now, of, on, one, only, or, other, out, over, said, see, she, so, some, than, the, their, them, then, there, these, they, this, time, to, up, use, very, was, we, were, what, when, where, which, who, will, with, words, would, you, your.

EVEN MORE WORDS

This title actually includes far more than 100 words due to the fact that you can use most of these words to build rhyming word families. Just a few examples:

an: can, fan, man
and: band, hand
at: bat, cat, hat, sat
but: cut, hut, nut
by: fly, shy, try, why
call: ball, fall, hall
did: bid, hid, lid, rid
each: beach, teach
find: bind, kind, mind
get: jet, let, met, net
in: fin, pin, tin, win
like: bike, hike, trike
look: book, took
may: day, hay, lay
more: for, sore, store
now: cow, how, pow
see: bee, knee, tree

Look for our complete line of Rainbow Word titles for more sight word fun!

www.MrKindergarten.com

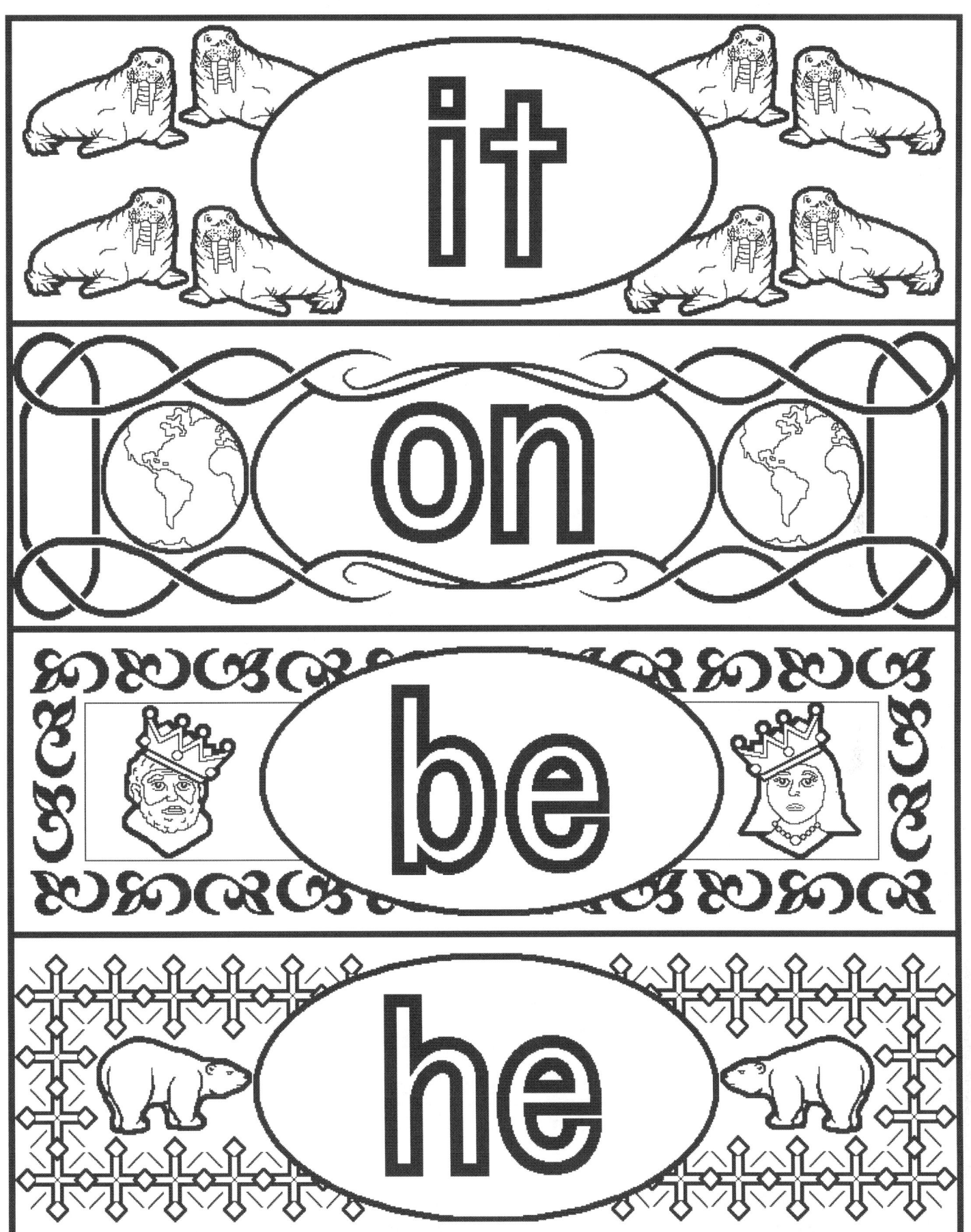

SIGHT WORD BRACELETS

www.MisterKindergarten.com ©2015 Dwayne Douglas Kohn

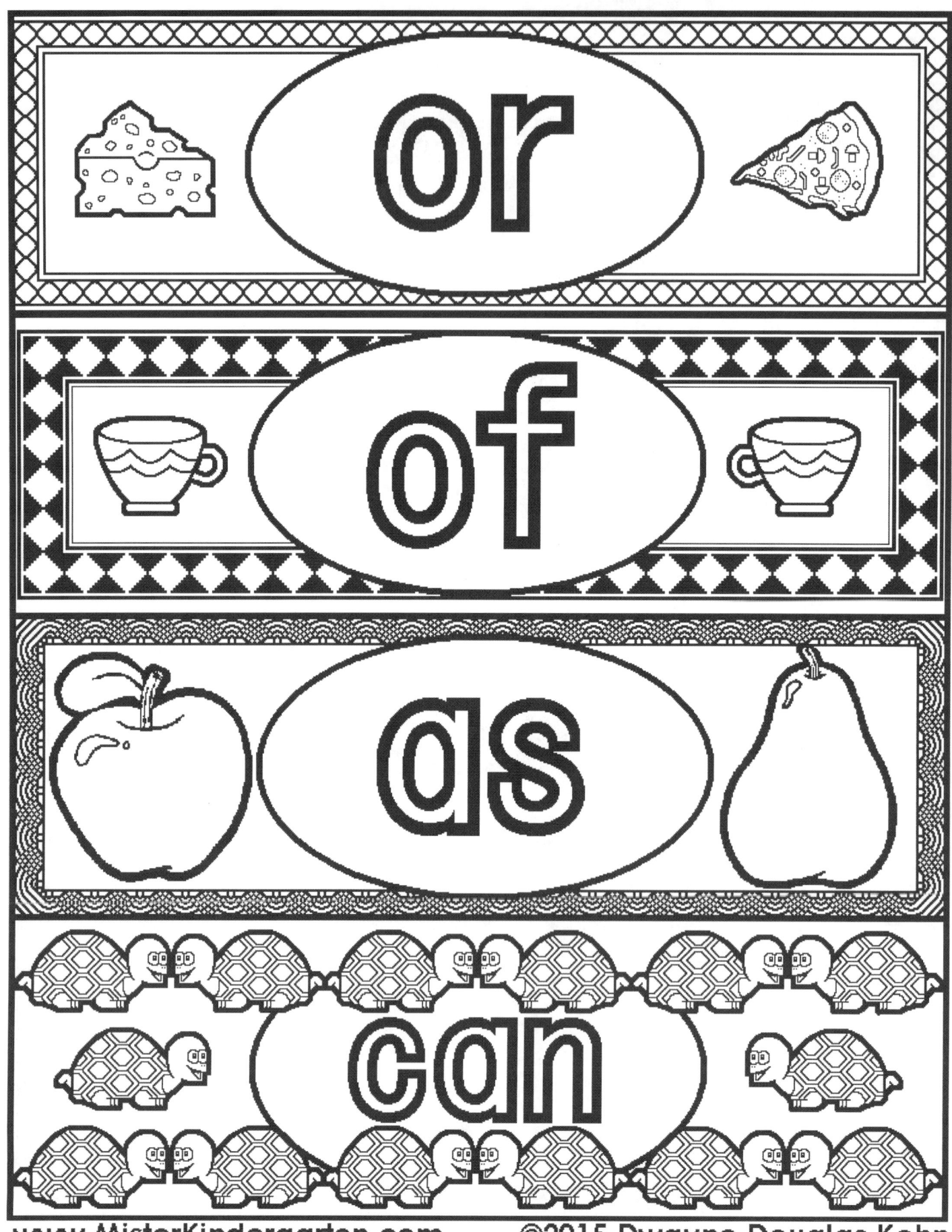

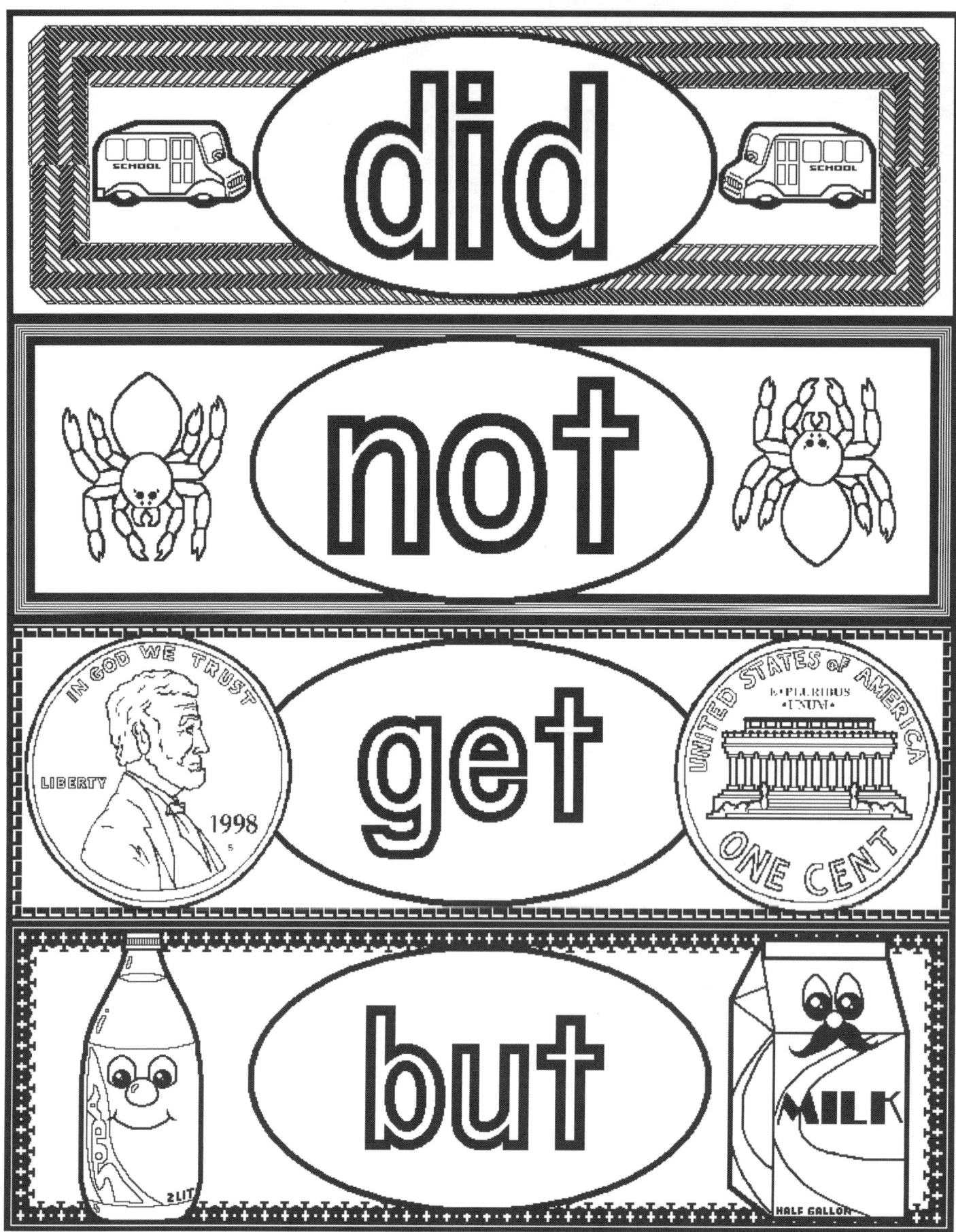

SIGHT WORD BRACELETS

www.MisterKindergarten.com ©2015 Dwayne Douglas Kohn

SIGHT WORD BRACELETS

www.MisterKindergarten.com ©2015 Dwayne Douglas Kohn

SIGHT WORD BRACELETS

www.MisterKindergarten.com ©2015 Dwayne Douglas Kohn

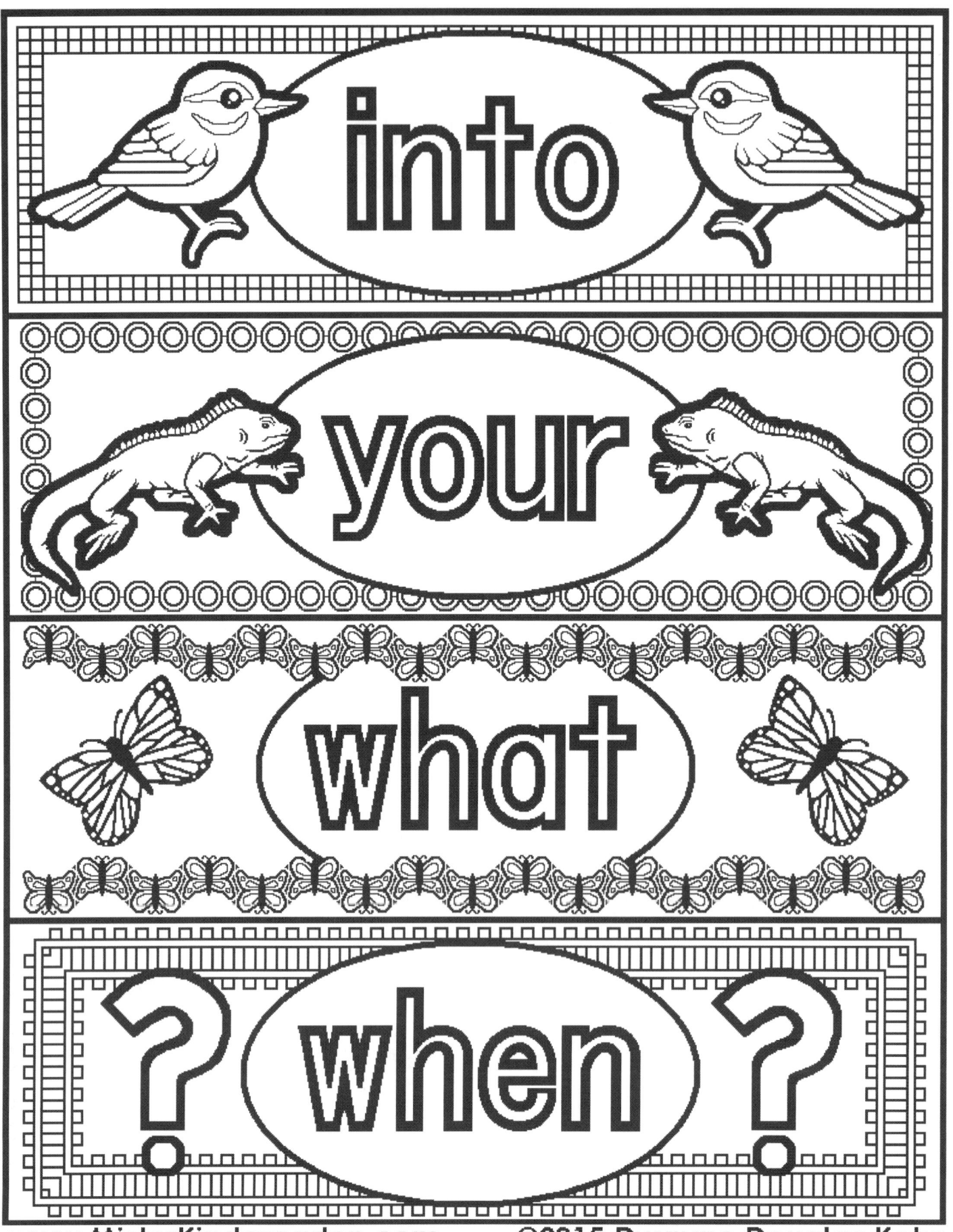

SIGHT WORD BRACELETS

www.MisterKindergarten.com ©2015 Dwayne Douglas Kohn

SIGHT WORD BRACELETS

www.MisterKindergarten.com ©2015 Dwayne Douglas Kohn

SIGHT WORD BRACELETS

www.MisterKindergarten.com ©2015 Dwayne Douglas Kohn

SIGHT WORD BRACELETS

SIGHT WORD BRACELETS

be

be

be

be

www.MisterKindergarten.com ©2015 Dwayne Douglas Kohn

SIGHT WORD BRACELETS

been

been

been

been

www.MisterKindergarten.com ©2015 Dwayne Douglas Kohn

SIGHT WORD BRACELETS

but

but

but

but

www.MisterKindergarten.com ©2015 Dwayne Douglas Kohn

SIGHT WORD BRACELETS

by

by

by

by

www.MisterKindergarten.com ©2015 Dwayne Douglas Kohn

SIGHT WORD BRACELETS

call

call

call

call

www.MisterKindergarten.com ©2015 Dwayne Douglas Kohn

SIGHT WORD BRACELETS

can

can

can

can

www.MisterKindergarten.com   ©2015 Dwayne Douglas Kohn

SIGHT WORD BRACELETS

come

come

come

come

www.MisterKindergarten.com ©2015 Dwayne Douglas Kohn

SIGHT WORD BRACELETS

could

could

could

could

www.MisterKindergarten.com ©2015 Dwayne Douglas Kohn

SIGHT WORD BRACELETS

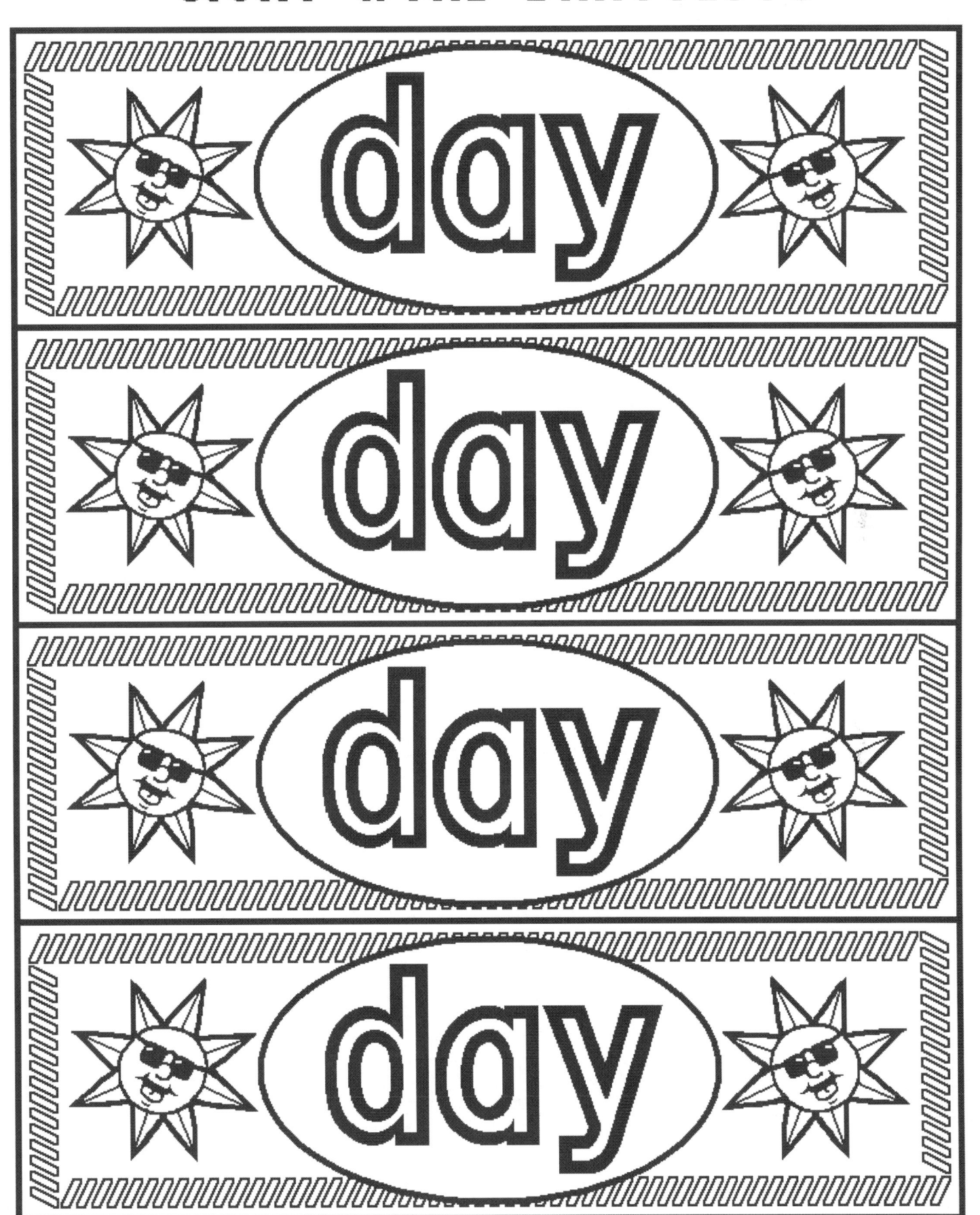

day

day

day

day

www.MisterKindergarten.com ©2015 Dwayne Douglas Kohn

SIGHT WORD BRACELETS

did

did

did

did

www.MisterKindergarten.com ©2015 Dwayne Douglas Kohn

SIGHT WORD BRACELETS

do

do

do

do

www.MisterKindergarten.com ©2015 Dwayne Douglas Kohn

SIGHT WORD BRACELETS

down

down

down

down

www.MisterKindergarten.com ©2015 Dwayne Douglas Kohn

SIGHT WORD BRACELETS

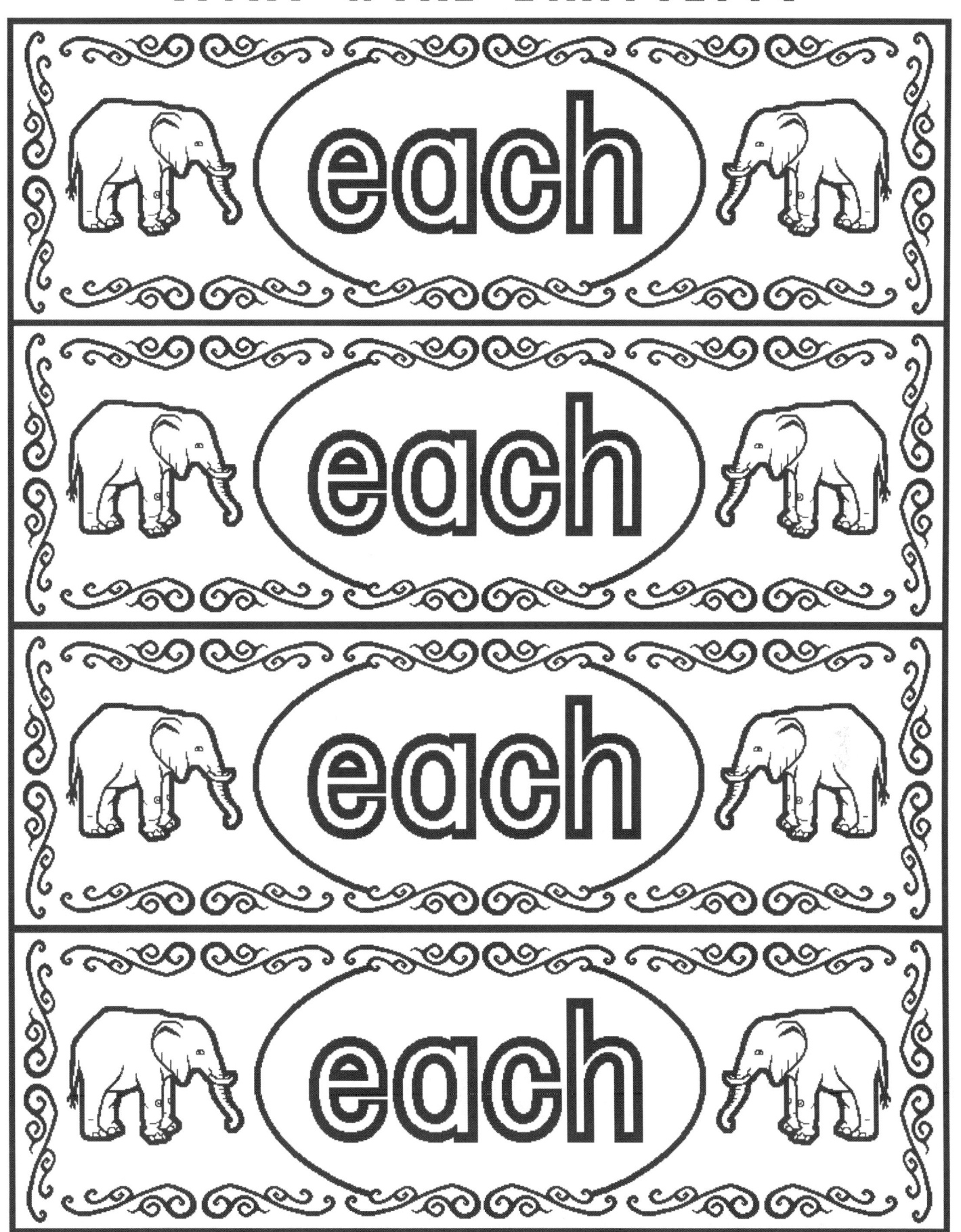

each

each

each

each

www.MisterKindergarten.com ©2015 Dwayne Douglas Kohn

SIGHT WORD BRACELETS

find

find

find

find

www.MisterKindergarten.com ©2015 Dwayne Douglas Kohn

SIGHT WORD BRACELETS

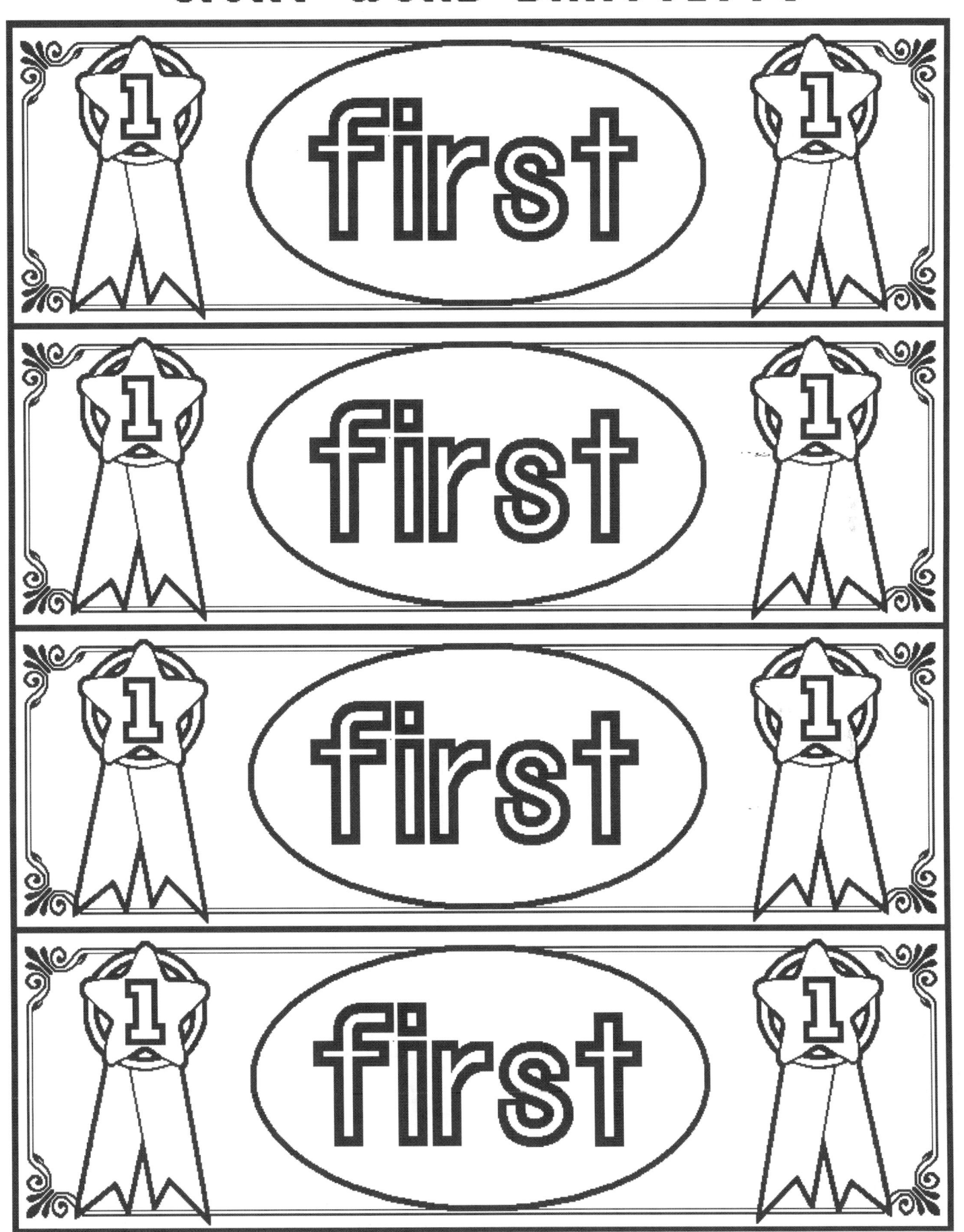

first

first

first

first

www.MisterKindergarten.com ©2015 Dwayne Douglas Kohn

SIGHT WORD BRACELETS

for

for

for

for

www.MisterKindergarten.com ©2015 Dwayne Douglas Kohn

SIGHT WORD BRACELETS

from

from

from

from

www.MisterKindergarten.com ©2015 Dwayne Douglas Kohn

SIGHT WORD BRACELETS

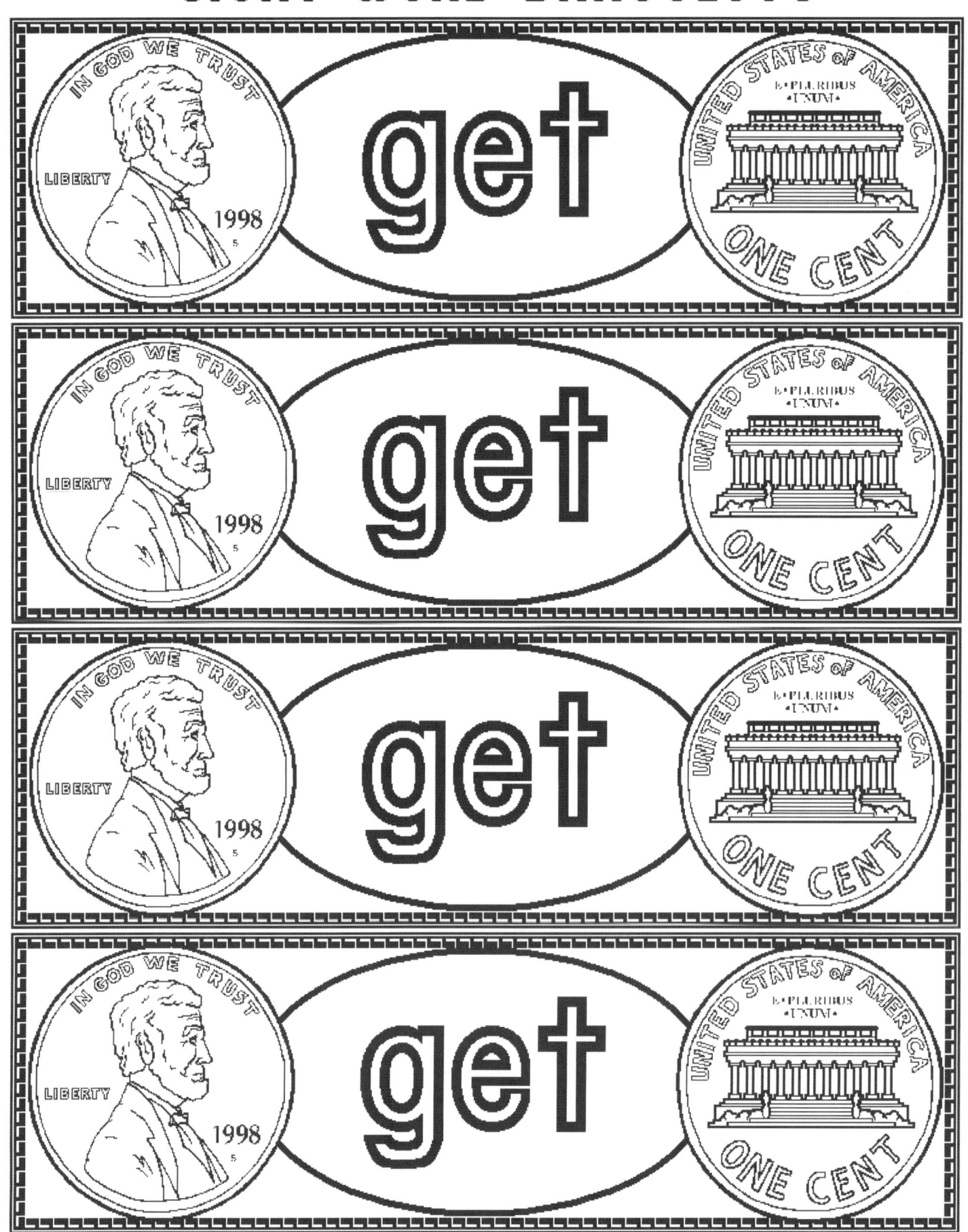

get

get

get

get

www.MisterKindergarten.com ©2015 Dwayne Douglas Kohn

SIGHT WORD BRACELETS

go

go

go

go

www.MisterKindergarten.com ©2015 Dwayne Douglas Kohn

SIGHT WORD BRACELETS

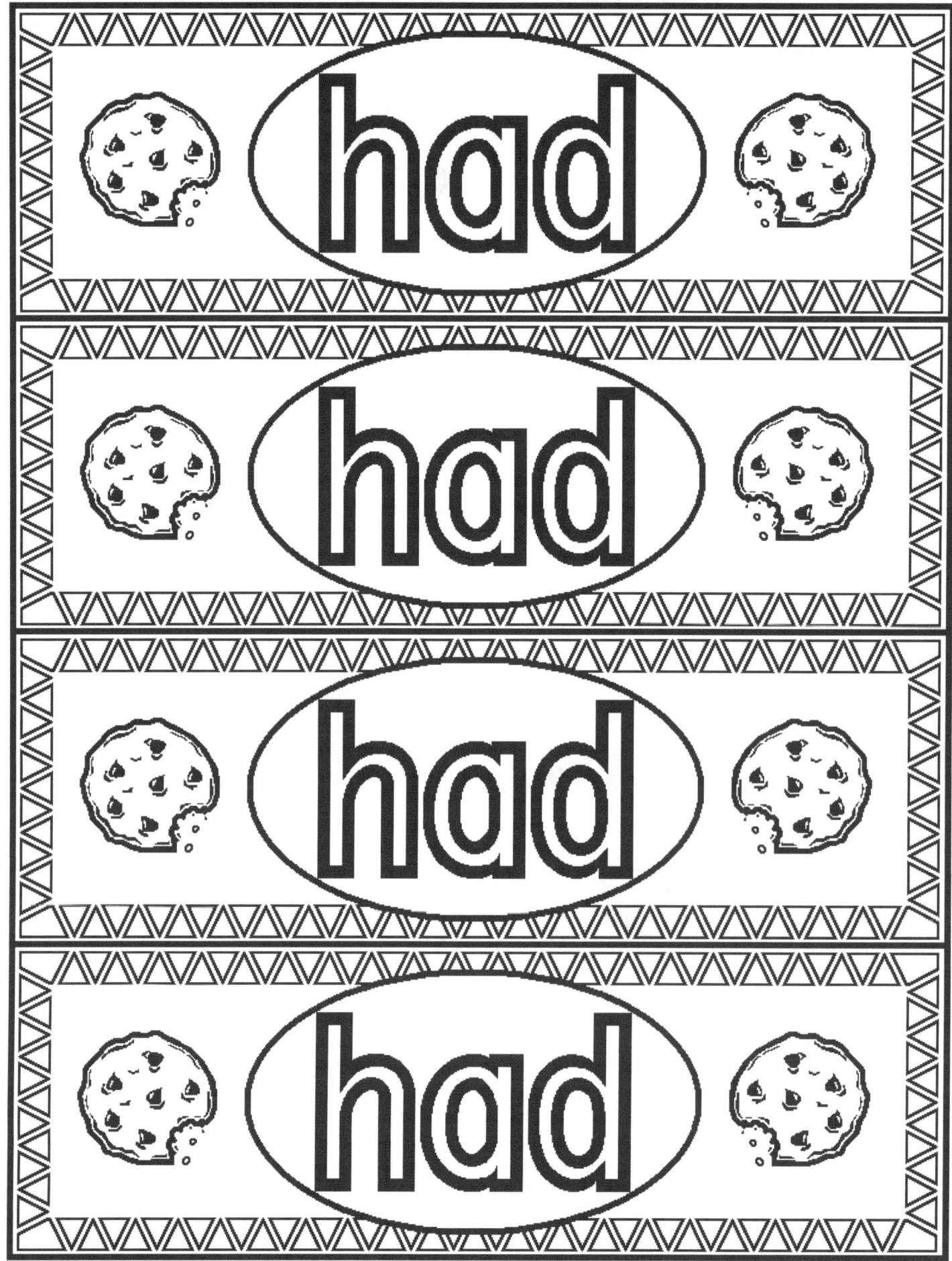

had

had

had

had

www.MisterKindergarten.com ©2015 Dwayne Douglas Kohn

SIGHT WORD BRACELETS

has

has

has

has

www.MisterKindergarten.com   ©2015 Dwayne Douglas Kohn

SIGHT WORD BRACELETS

have

have

have

have

www.MisterKindergarten.com ©2015 Dwayne Douglas Kohn

SIGHT WORD BRACELETS

he

he

he

he

www.MisterKindergarten.com ©2015 Dwayne Douglas Kohn

SIGHT WORD BRACELETS

her

her

her

her

www.MisterKindergarten.com ©2015 Dwayne Douglas Kohn

SIGHT WORD BRACELETS

him

him

him

him

www.MisterKindergarten.com ©2015 Dwayne Douglas Kohn

SIGHT WORD BRACELETS

his

his

his

his

www.MisterKindergarten.com ©2015 Dwayne Douglas Kohn

SIGHT WORD BRACELETS

how

how

how

how

www.MisterKindergarten.com ©2015 Dwayne Douglas Kohn

SIGHT WORD BRACELETS

I

I

I

I

www.MisterKindergarten.com ©2015 Dwayne Douglas Kohn

SIGHT WORD BRACELETS

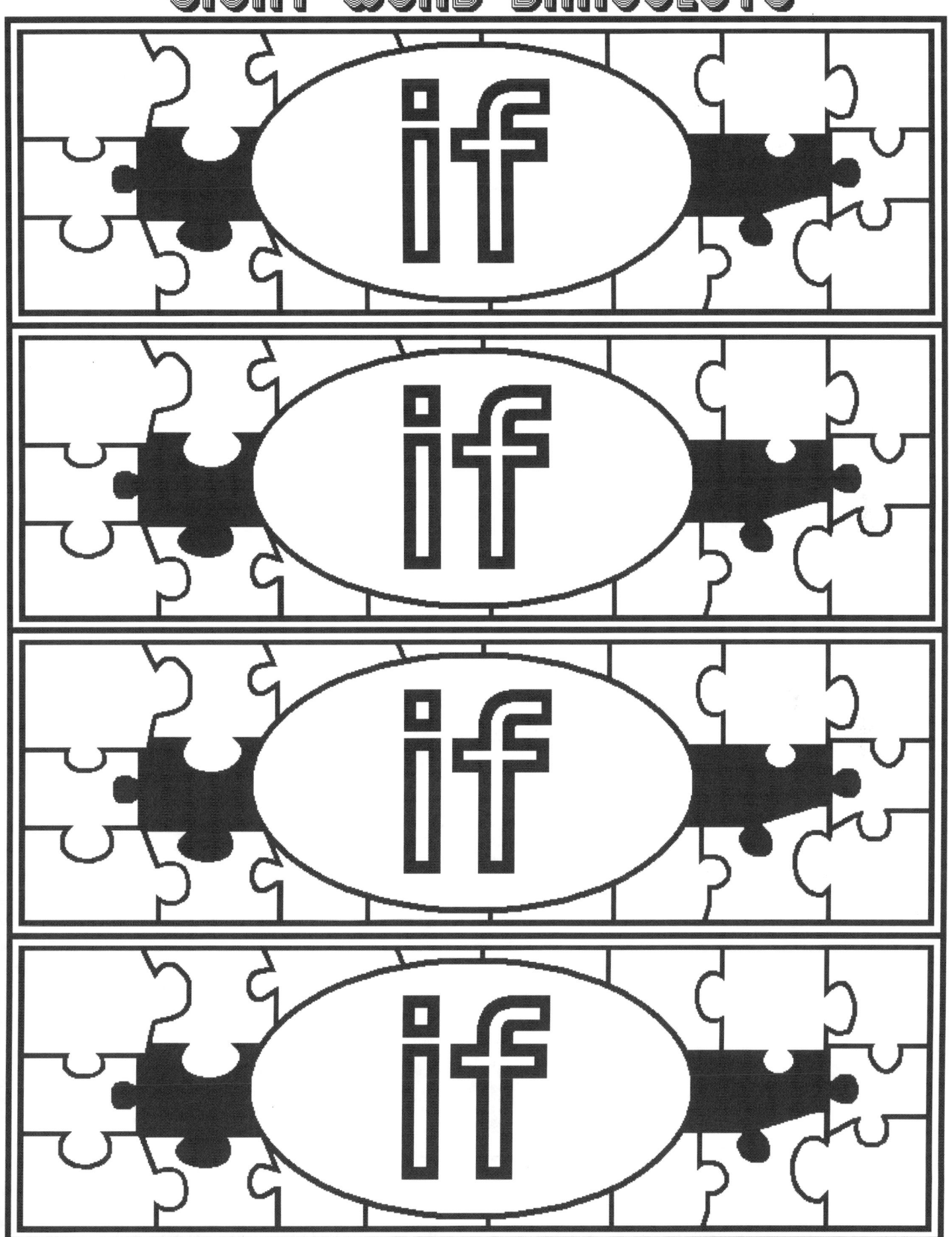

if

if

if

if

www.MisterKindergarten.com ©2015 Dwayne Douglas Kohn

SIGHT WORD BRACELETS

in

in

in

in

www.MisterKindergarten.com ©2015 Dwayne Douglas Kohn

SIGHT WORD BRACELETS

into

into

into

into

www.MisterKindergarten.com ©2015 Dwayne Douglas Kohn

SIGHT WORD BRACELETS

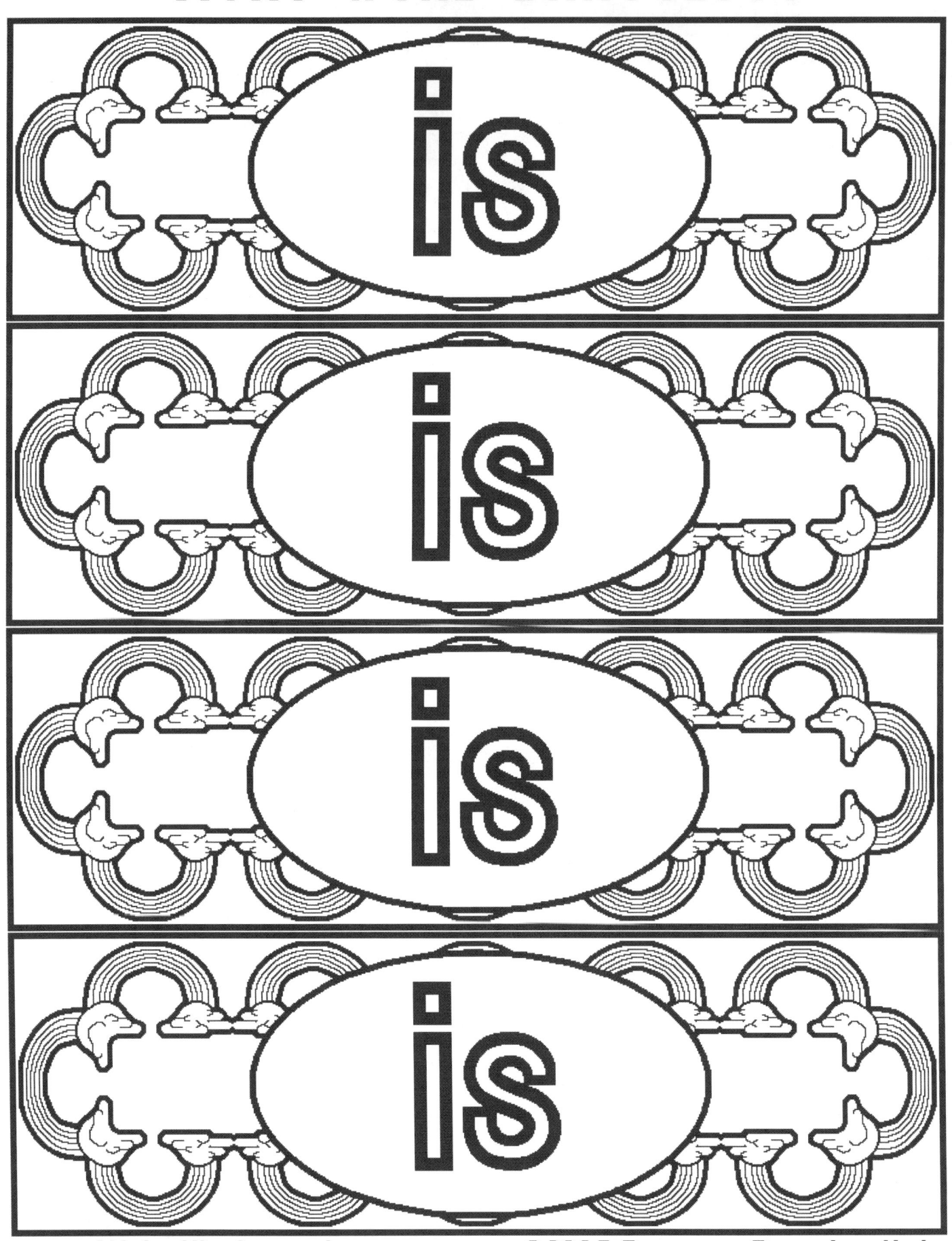

is

is

is

is

www.MisterKindergarten.com ©2015 Dwayne Douglas Kohn

SIGHT WORD BRACELETS

it

it

it

it

www.MisterKindergarten.com ©2015 Dwayne Douglas Kohn

SIGHT WORD BRACELETS

its

its

its

its

www.MisterKindergarten.com ©2015 Dwayne Douglas Kohn

SIGHT WORD BRACELETS

just

just

just

just

www.MisterKindergarten.com ©2015 Dwayne Douglas Kohn

SIGHT WORD BRACELETS

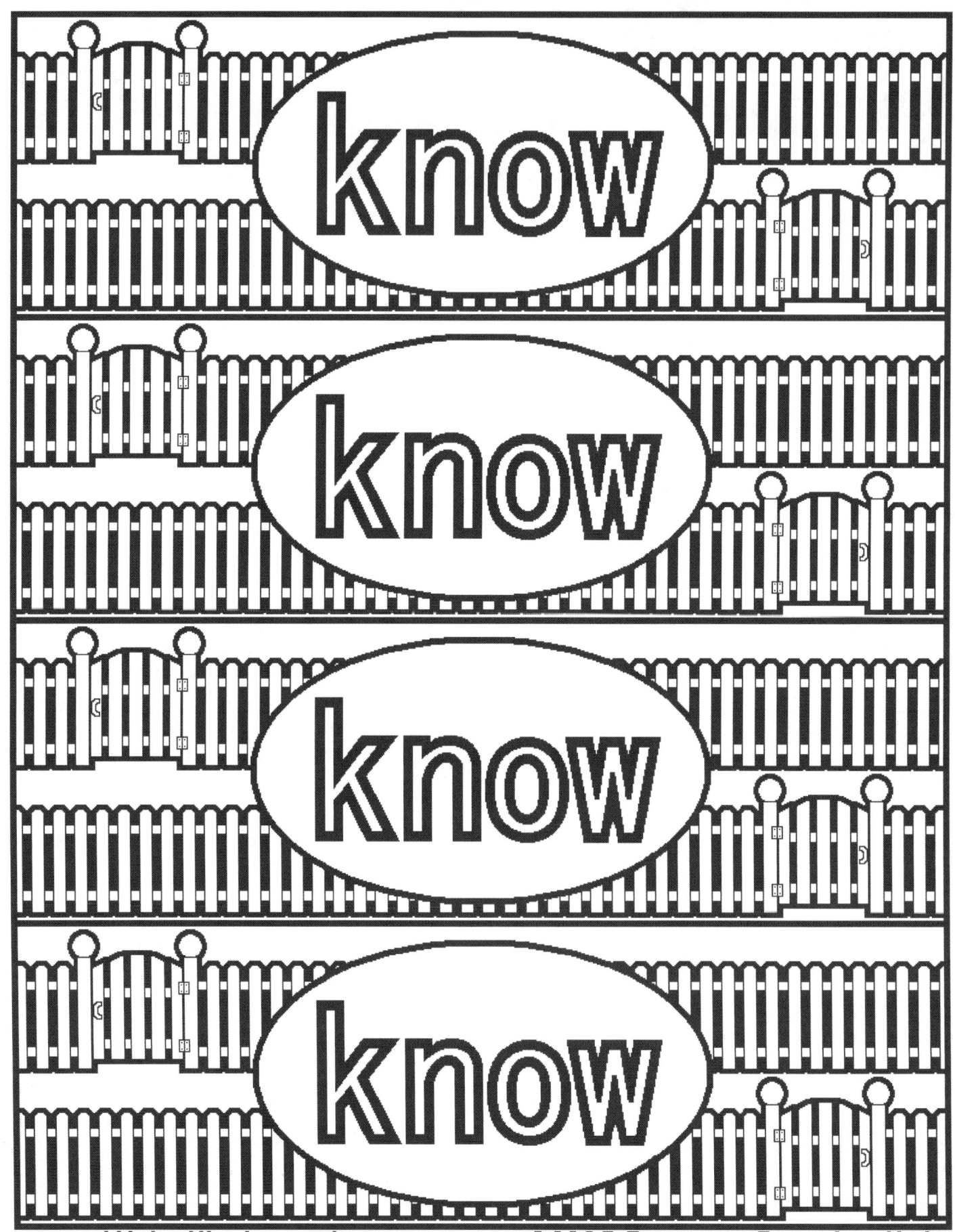

know

know

know

know

www.MisterKindergarten.com ©2015 Dwayne Douglas Kohn

SIGHT WORD BRACELETS

like

like

like

like

www.MisterKindergarten.com ©2015 Dwayne Douglas Kohn

SIGHT WORD BRACELETS

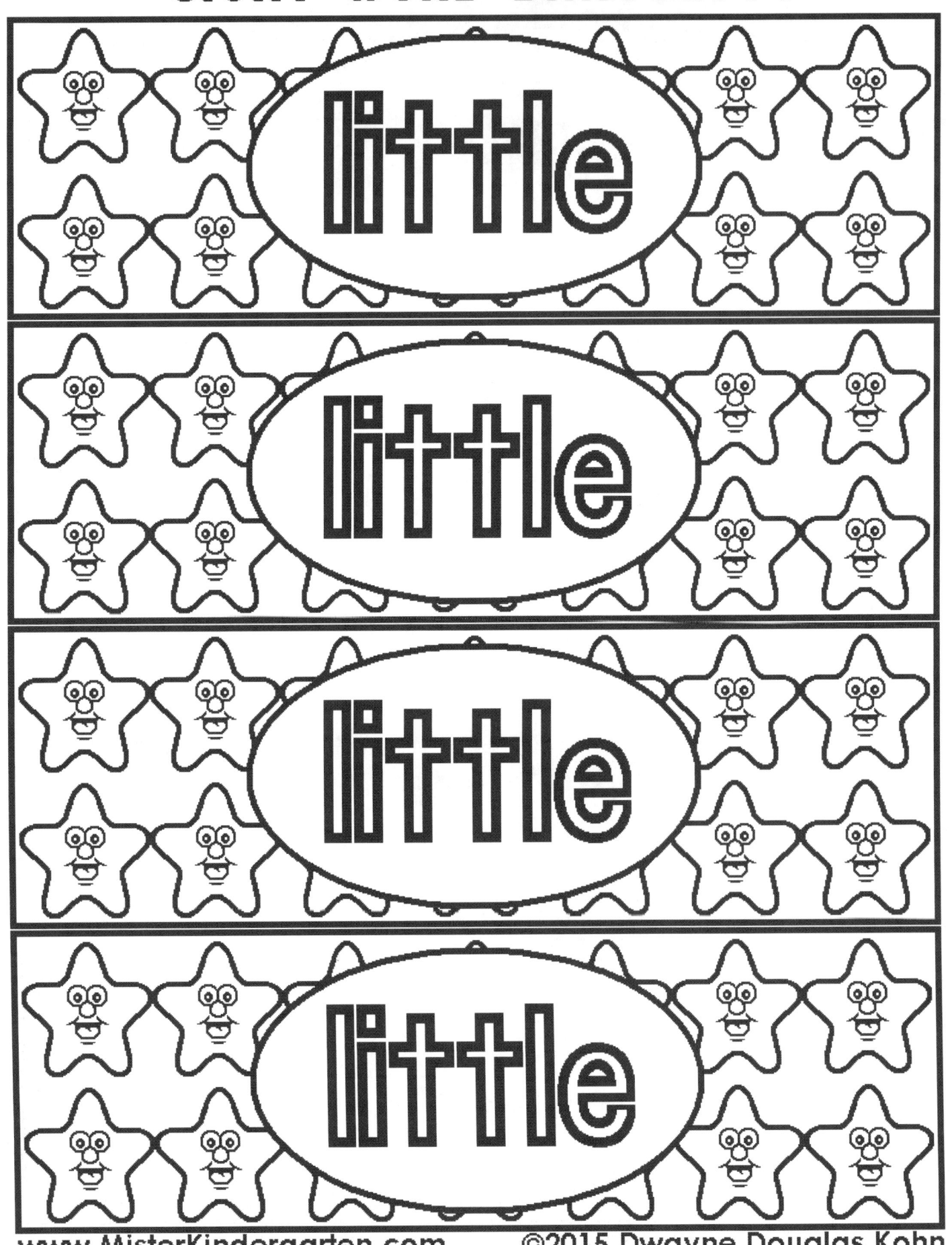

little

little

little

little

www.MisterKindergarten.com ©2015 Dwayne Douglas Kohn

SIGHT WORD BRACELETS

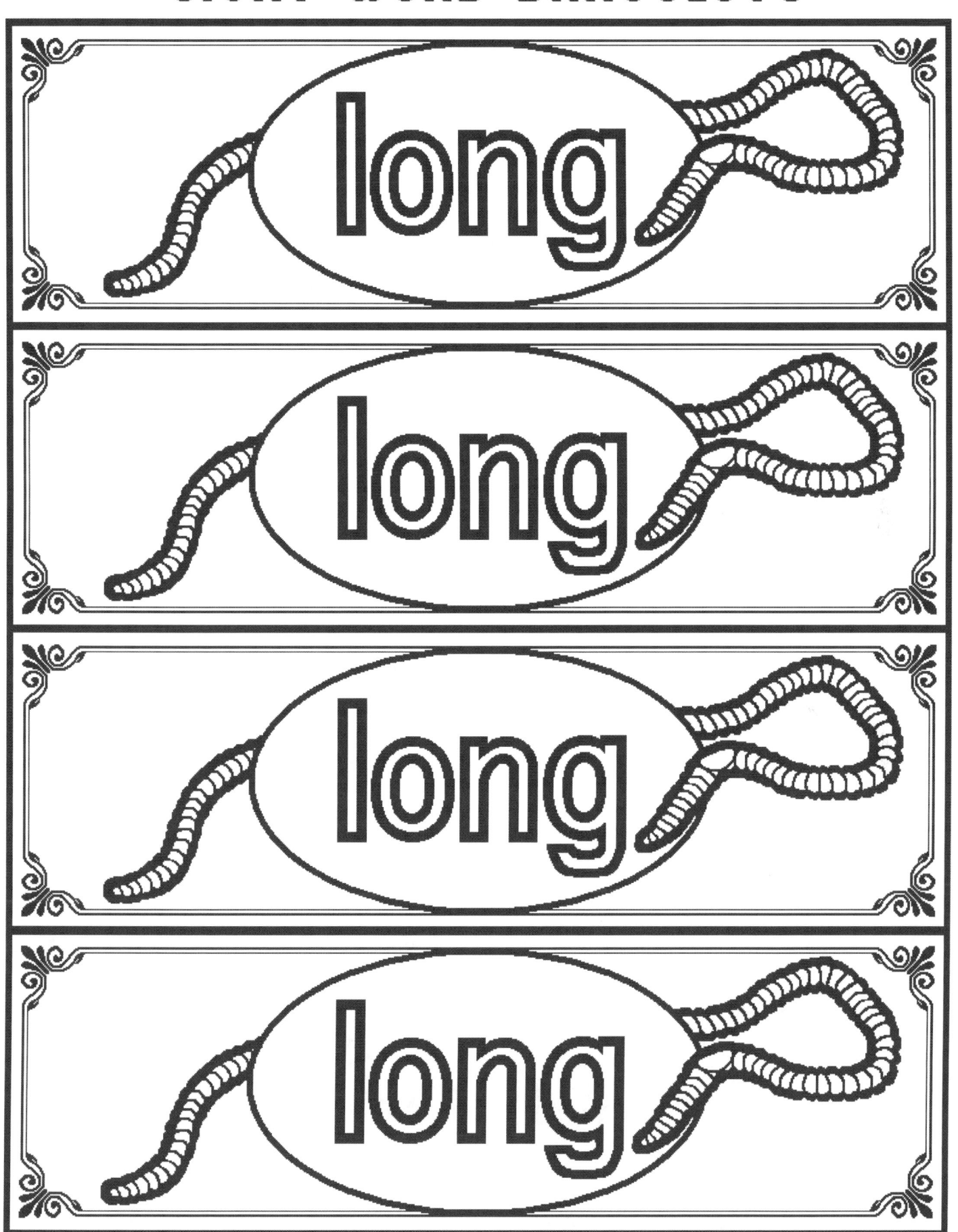

long

long

long

long

www.MisterKindergarten.com ©2015 Dwayne Douglas Kohn

SIGHT WORD BRACELETS

look

look

look

look

www.MisterKindergarten.com ©2015 Dwayne Douglas Kohn

SIGHT WORD BRACELETS

made

made

made

made

www.MisterKindergarten.com ©2015 Dwayne Douglas Kohn

SIGHT WORD BRACELETS

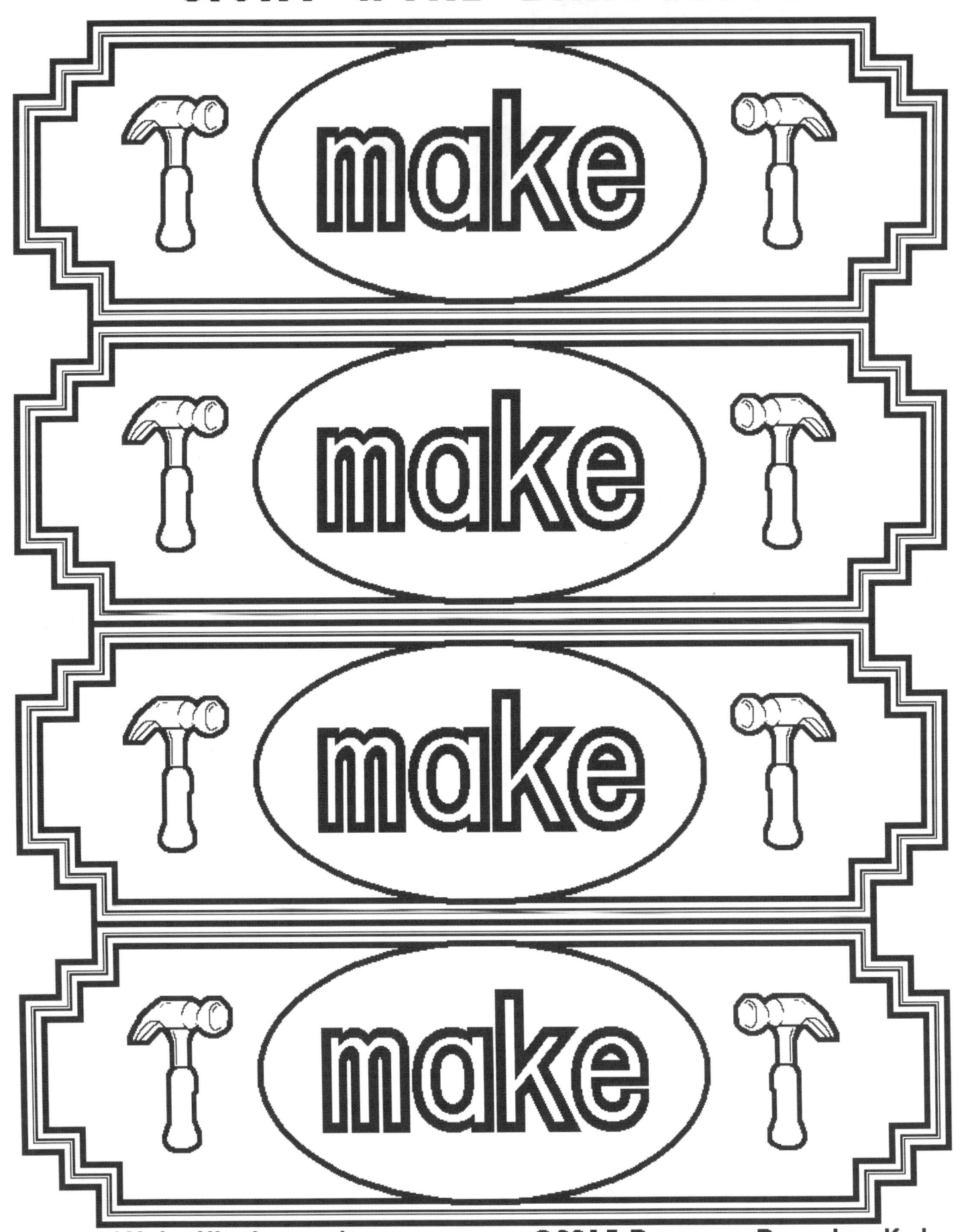

make

make

make

make

www.MisterKindergarten.com ©2015 Dwayne Douglas Kohn

SIGHT WORD BRACELETS

many

many

many

many

www.MisterKindergarten.com   ©2015 Dwayne Douglas Kohn

SIGHT WORD BRACELETS

may

may

may

may

www.MisterKindergarten.com ©2015 Dwayne Douglas Kohn

SIGHT WORD BRACELETS

more

more

more

more

www.MisterKindergarten.com ©2015 Dwayne Douglas Kohn

SIGHT WORD BRACELETS

most

most

most

most

www.MisterKindergarten.com ©2015 Dwayne Douglas Kohn

SIGHT WORD BRACELETS

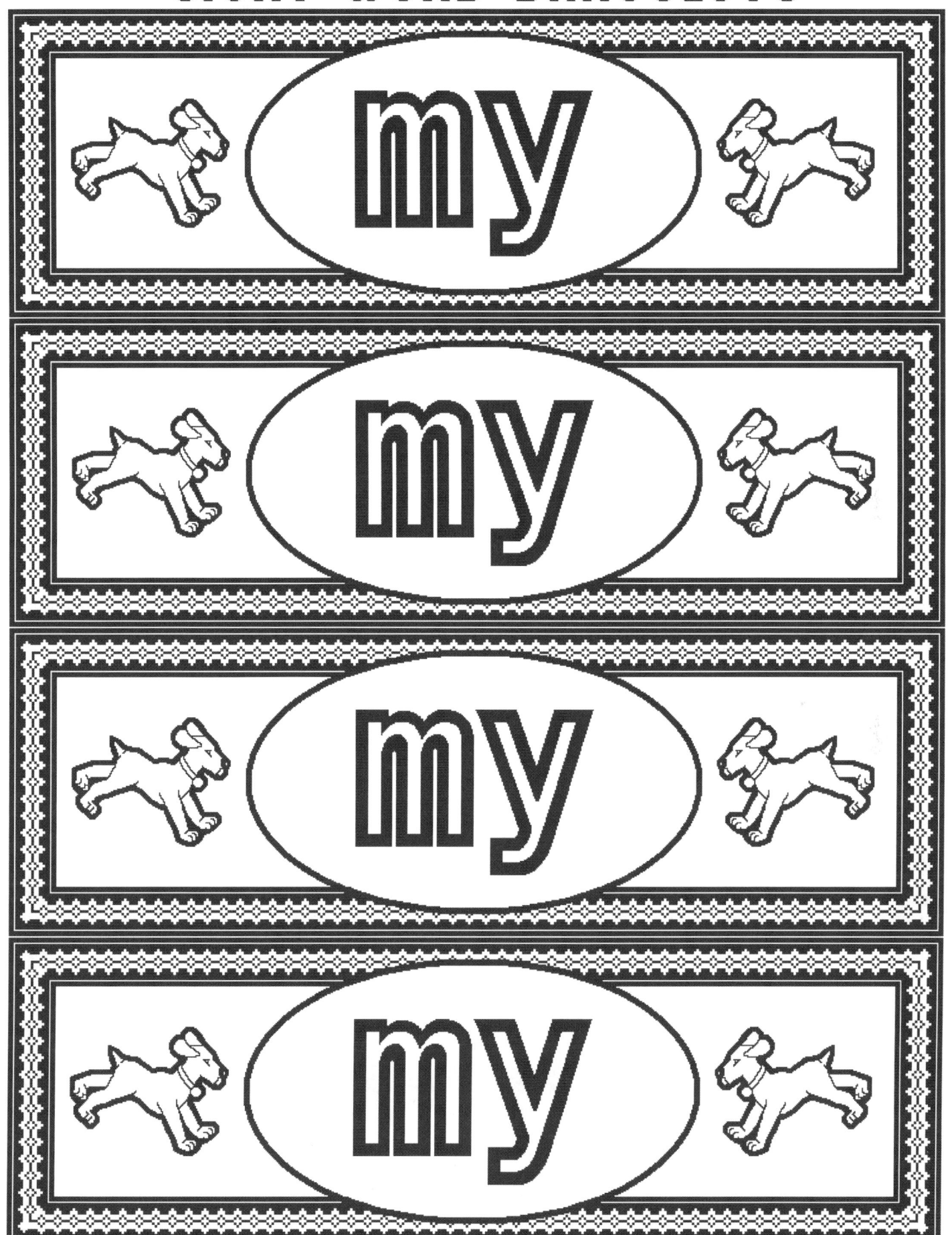

my

my

my

my

www.MisterKindergarten.com ©2015 Dwayne Douglas Kohn

SIGHT WORD BRACELETS

no

no

no

no

www.MisterKindergarten.com ©2015 Dwayne Douglas Kohn

SIGHT WORD BRACELETS

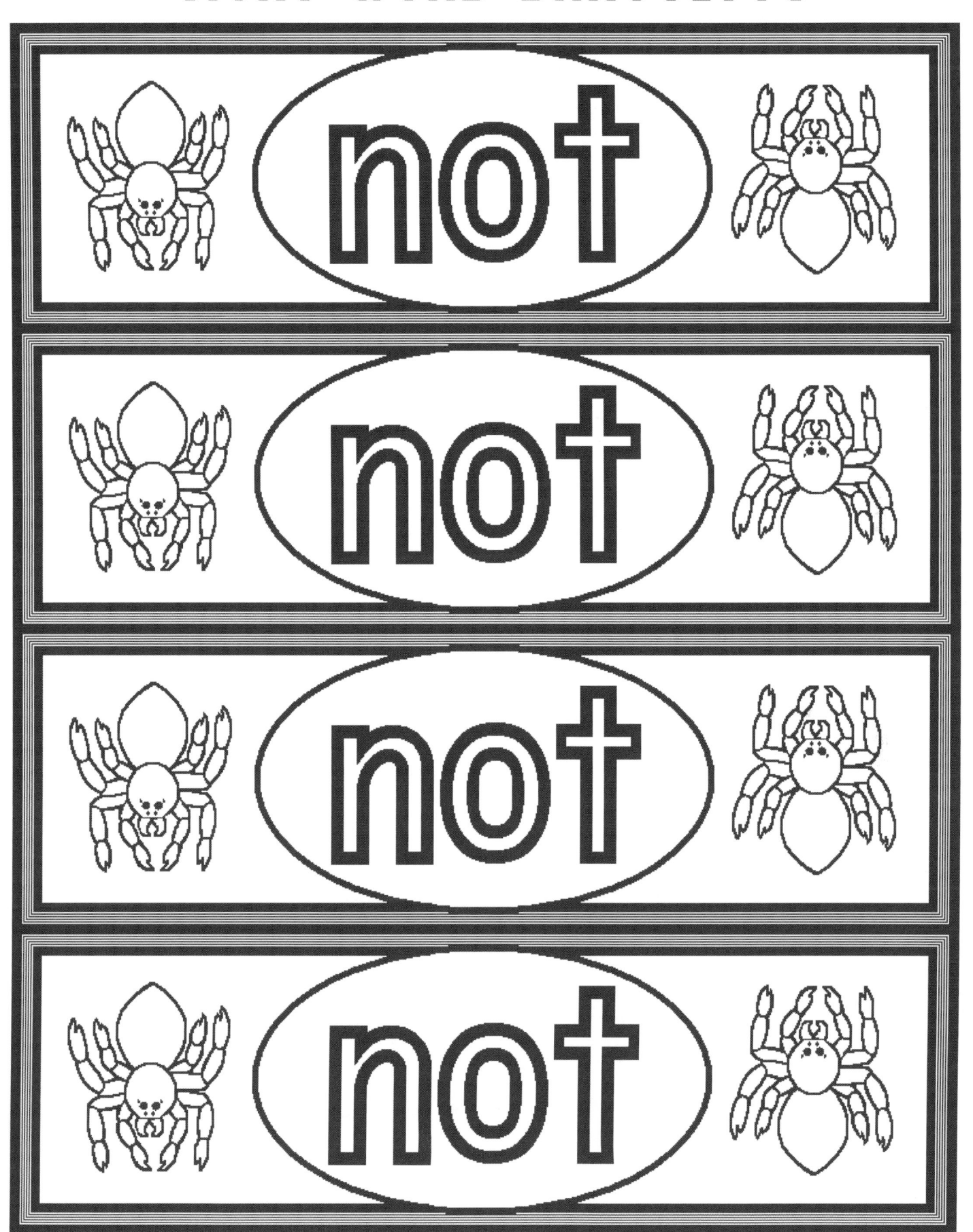

not

not

not

not

www.MisterKindergarten.com ©2015 Dwayne Douglas Kohn

SIGHT WORD BRACELETS

now

now

now

now

www.MisterKindergarten.com ©2015 Dwayne Douglas Kohn

SIGHT WORD BRACELETS

of

of

of

of

www.MisterKindergarten.com ©2015 Dwayne Douglas Kohn

SIGHT WORD BRACELETS

on

on

on

on

www.MisterKindergarten.com   ©2015 Dwayne Douglas Kohn

SIGHT WORD BRACELETS

one

one

one

one

www.MisterKindergarten.com ©2015 Dwayne Douglas Kohn

SIGHT WORD BRACELETS

only

only

only

only

www.MisterKindergarten.com ©2015 Dwayne Douglas Kohn

SIGHT WORD BRACELETS

or

or

or

or

www.MisterKindergarten.com ©2015 Dwayne Douglas Kohn

SIGHT WORD BRACELETS

other

other

other

other

www.MisterKindergarten.com ©2015 Dwayne Douglas Kohn

SIGHT WORD BRACELETS

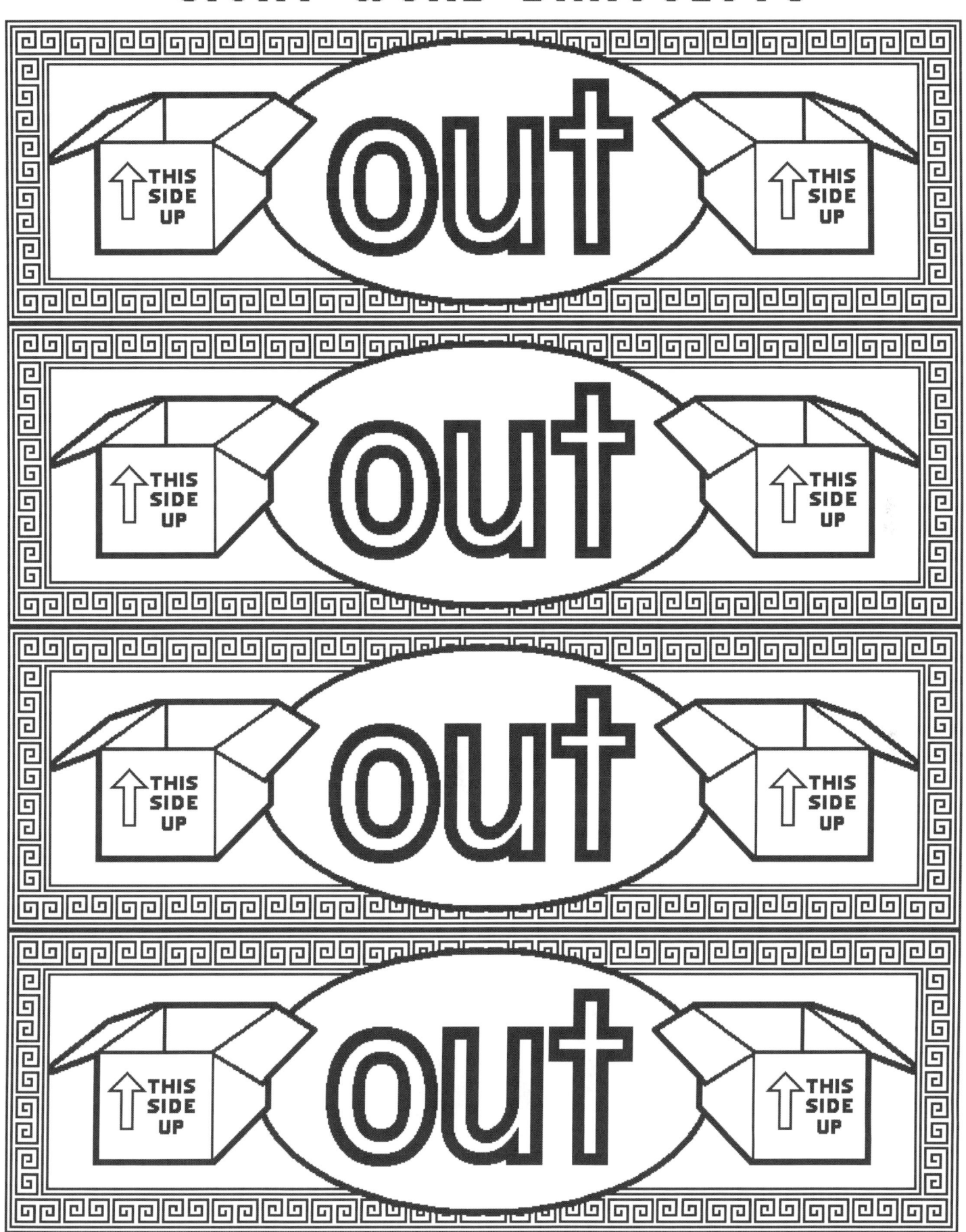

out

out

out

out

www.MisterKindergarten.com ©2015 Dwayne Douglas Kohn

SIGHT WORD BRACELETS

over

over

over

over

www.MisterKindergarten.com ©2015 Dwayne Douglas Kohn

SIGHT WORD BRACELETS

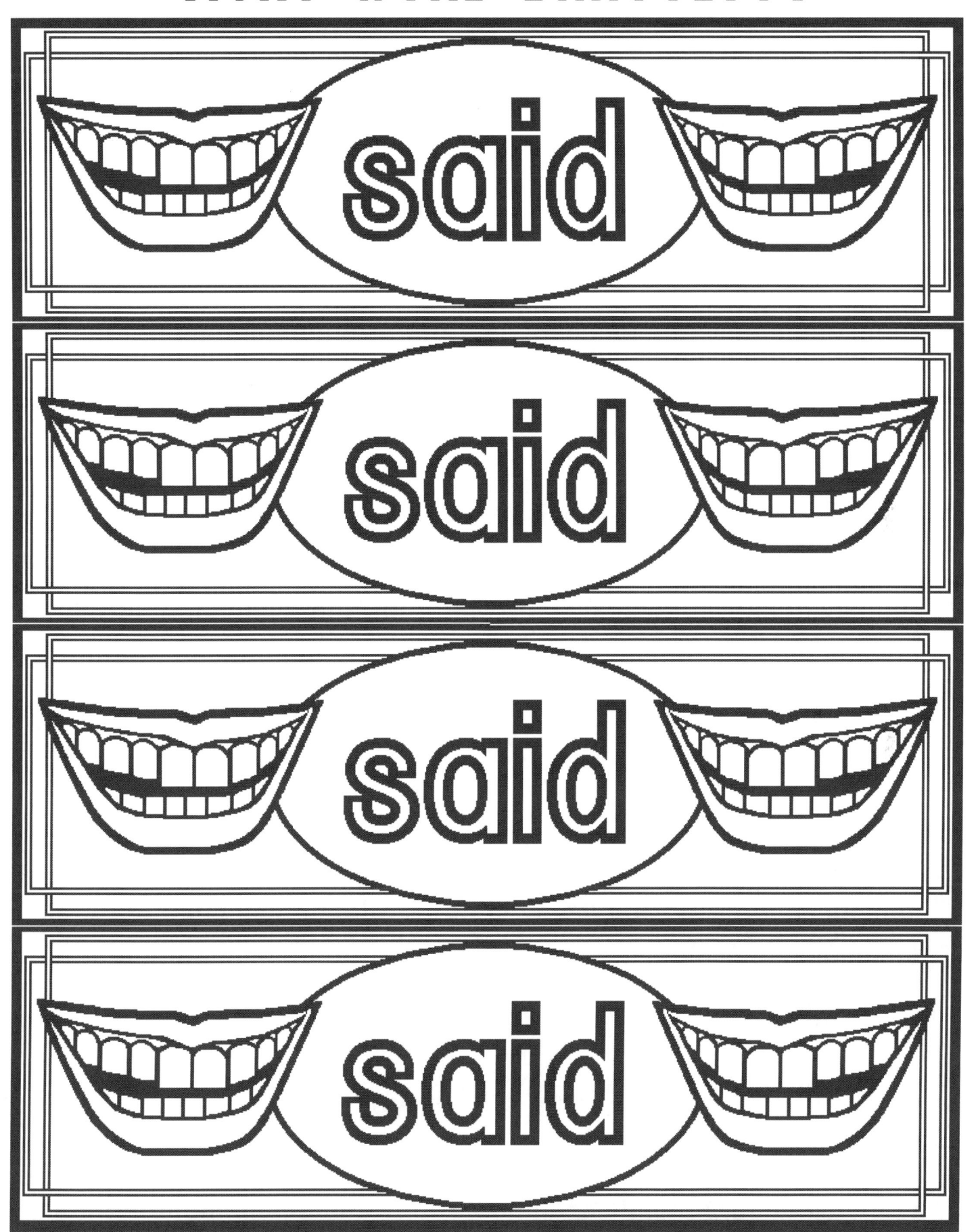

said

said

said

said

www.MisterKindergarten.com ©2015 Dwayne Douglas Kohn

SIGHT WORD BRACELETS

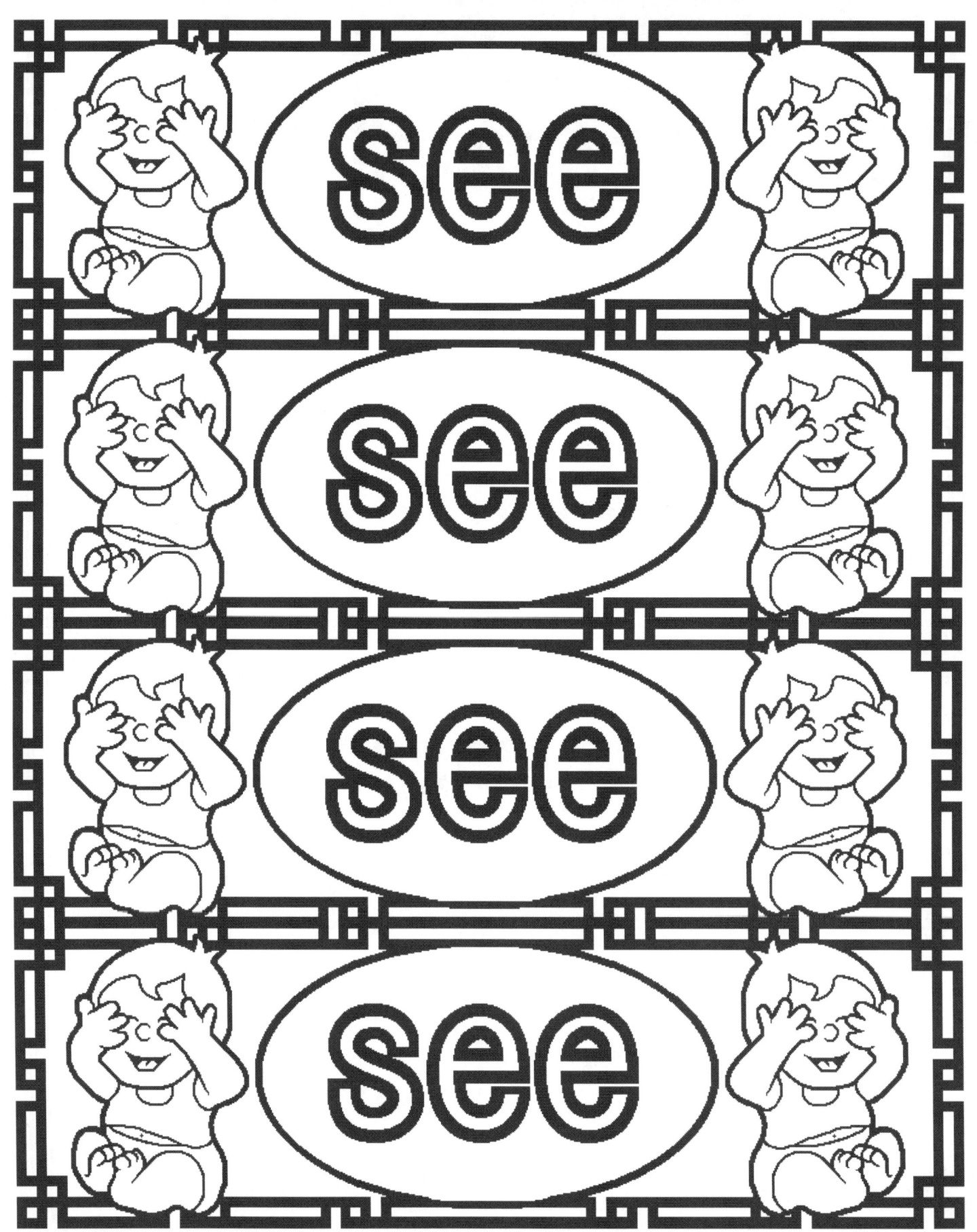

see

see

see

see

www.MisterKindergarten.com ©2015 Dwayne Douglas Kohn

SIGHT WORD BRACELETS

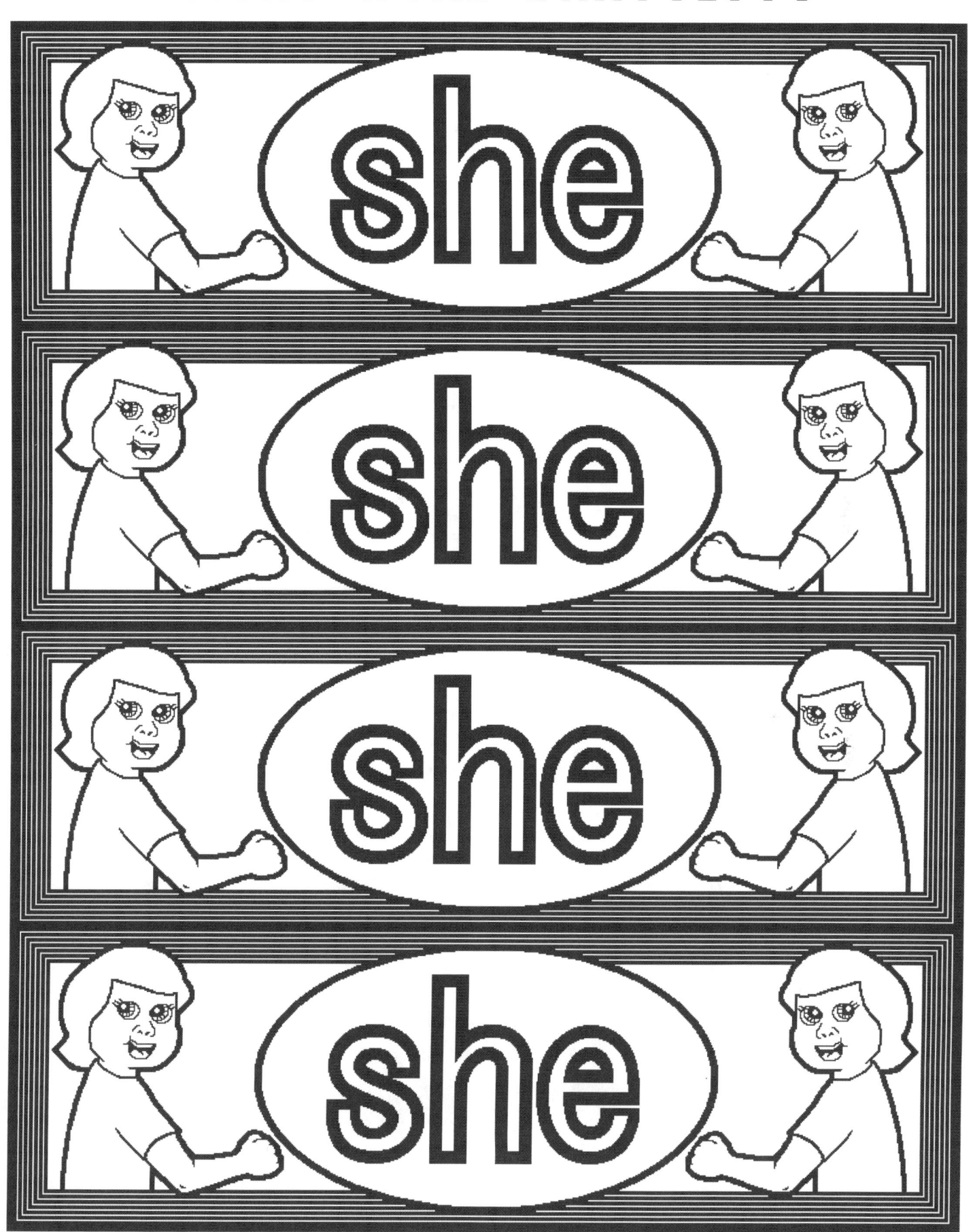

she

she

she

she

www.MisterKindergarten.com ©2015 Dwayne Douglas Kohn

SIGHT WORD BRACELETS

SO

SO

SO

SO

www.MisterKindergarten.com   ©2015 Dwayne Douglas Kohn

SIGHT WORD BRACELETS

some

some

some

some

www.MisterKindergarten.com ©2015 Dwayne Douglas Kohn

SIGHT WORD BRACELETS

than

than

than

than

www.MisterKindergarten.com © 2015 Dwayne Douglas Kohn

SIGHT WORD BRACELETS

the

the

the

the

www.MisterKindergarten.com ©2015 Dwayne Douglas Kohn

SIGHT WORD BRACELETS

their

their

their

their

www.MisterKindergarten.com ©2015 Dwayne Douglas Kohn

SIGHT WORD BRACELETS

them

them

them

them

www.MisterKindergarten.com ©2015 Dwayne Douglas Kohn

SIGHT WORD BRACELETS

then

then

then

then

www.MisterKindergarten.com ©2015 Dwayne Douglas Kohn

SIGHT WORD BRACELETS

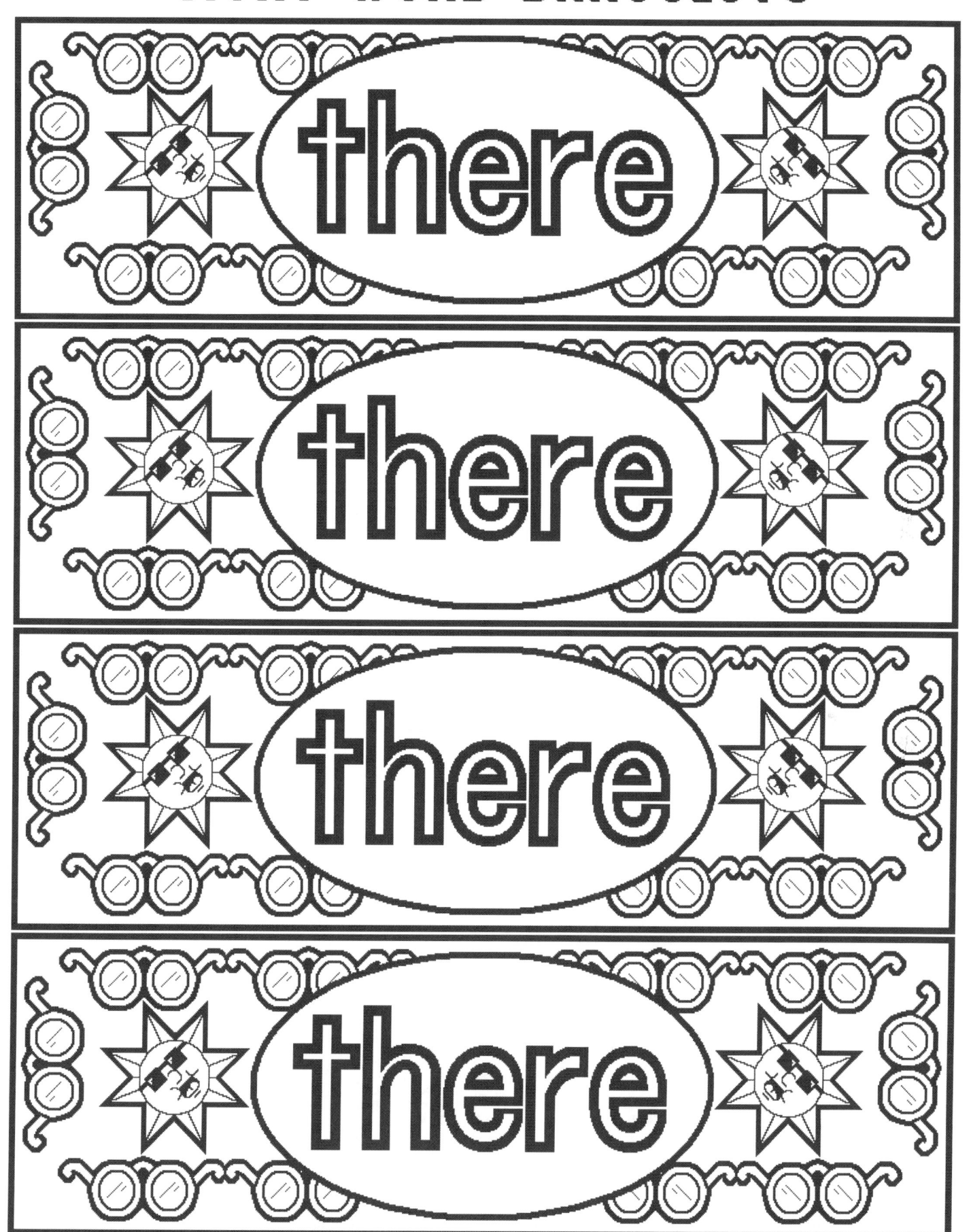

there

there

there

there

www.MisterKindergarten.com ©2015 Dwayne Douglas Kohn

SIGHT WORD BRACELETS

these

these

these

these

www.MisterKindergarten.com ©2015 Dwayne Douglas Kohn

SIGHT WORD BRACELETS

they

they

they

they

www.MisterKindergarten.com ©2015 Dwayne Douglas Kohn

SIGHT WORD BRACELETS

this

this

this

this

www.MisterKindergarten.com ©2015 Dwayne Douglas Kohn

SIGHT WORD BRACELETS

time

time

time

time

www.MisterKindergarten.com ©2015 Dwayne Douglas Kohn

SIGHT WORD BRACELETS

to

to

to

to

www.MisterKindergarten.com ©2015 Dwayne Douglas Kohn

SIGHT WORD BRACELETS

up

up

up

up

SIGHT WORD BRACELETS

use

use

use

use

www.MisterKindergarten.com ©2015 Dwayne Douglas Kohn

SIGHT WORD BRACELETS

very

very

very

very

www.MisterKindergarten.com ©2015 Dwayne Douglas Kohn

SIGHT WORD BRACELETS

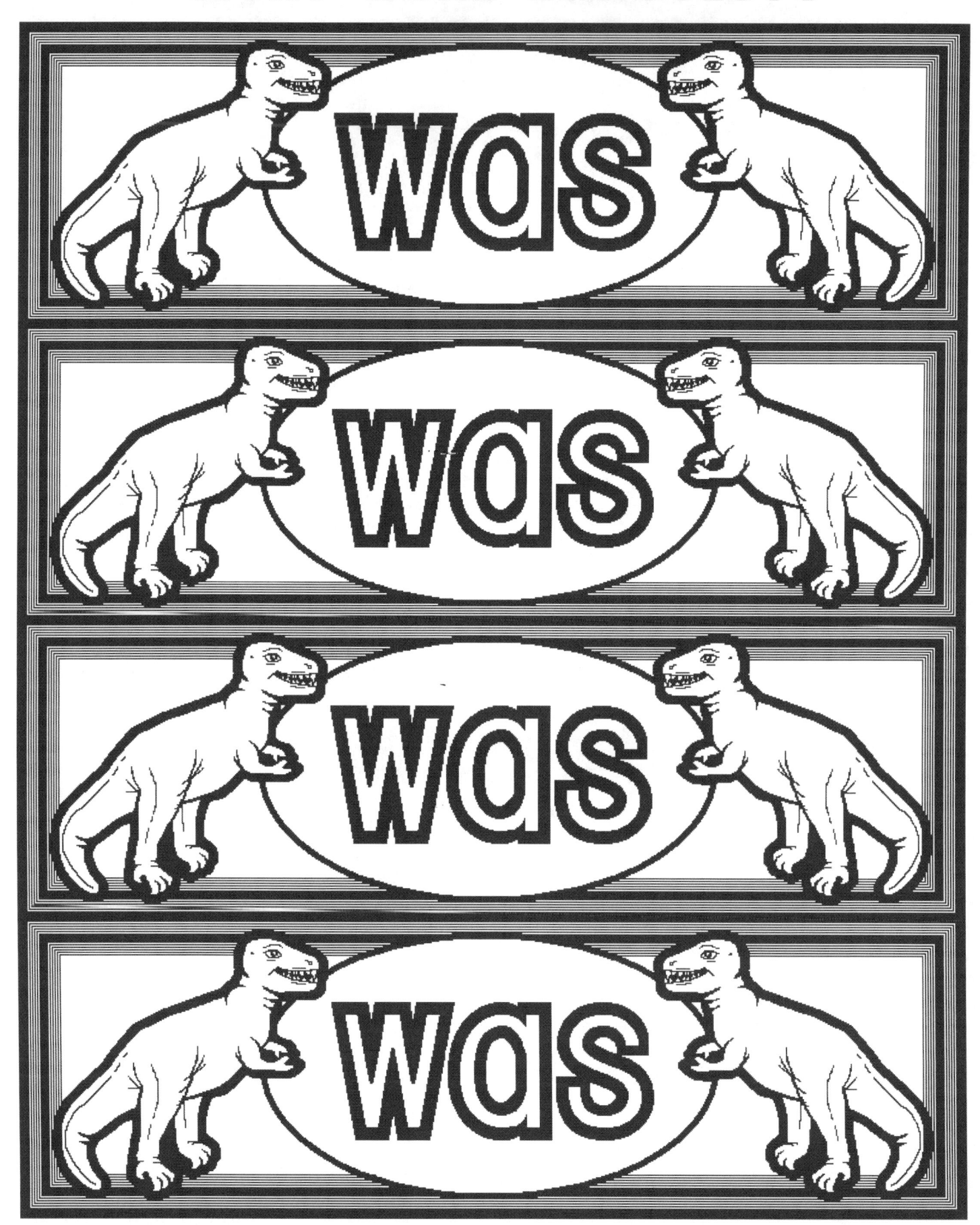

was

was

was

was

www.MisterKindergarten.com ©2015 Dwayne Douglas Kohn

SIGHT WORD BRACELETS

we

we

we

we

www.MisterKindergarten.com ©2015 Dwayne Douglas Kohn

SIGHT WORD BRACELETS

were

were

were

were

www.MisterKindergarten.com ©2015 Dwayne Douglas Kohn

SIGHT WORD BRACELETS

what

what

what

what

www.MisterKindergarten.com   ©2015 Dwayne Douglas Kohn

SIGHT WORD BRACELETS

? when ?

? when ?

? when ?

? when ?

www.MisterKindergarten.com ©2015 Dwayne Douglas Kohn

SIGHT WORD BRACELETS

where

where

where

where

www.MisterKindergarten.com ©2015 Dwayne Douglas Kohn

SIGHT WORD BRACELETS

which

which

which

which

www.MisterKindergarten.com ©2015 Dwayne Douglas Kohn

SIGHT WORD BRACELETS

who

who

who

who

www.MisterKindergarten.com ©2015 Dwayne Douglas Kohn

SIGHT WORD BRACELETS

will

will

will

will

www.MisterKindergarten.com ©2015 Dwayne Douglas Kohn

SIGHT WORD BRACELETS

with

with

with

with

www.MisterKindergarten.com ©2015 Dwayne Douglas Kohn

SIGHT WORD BRACELETS

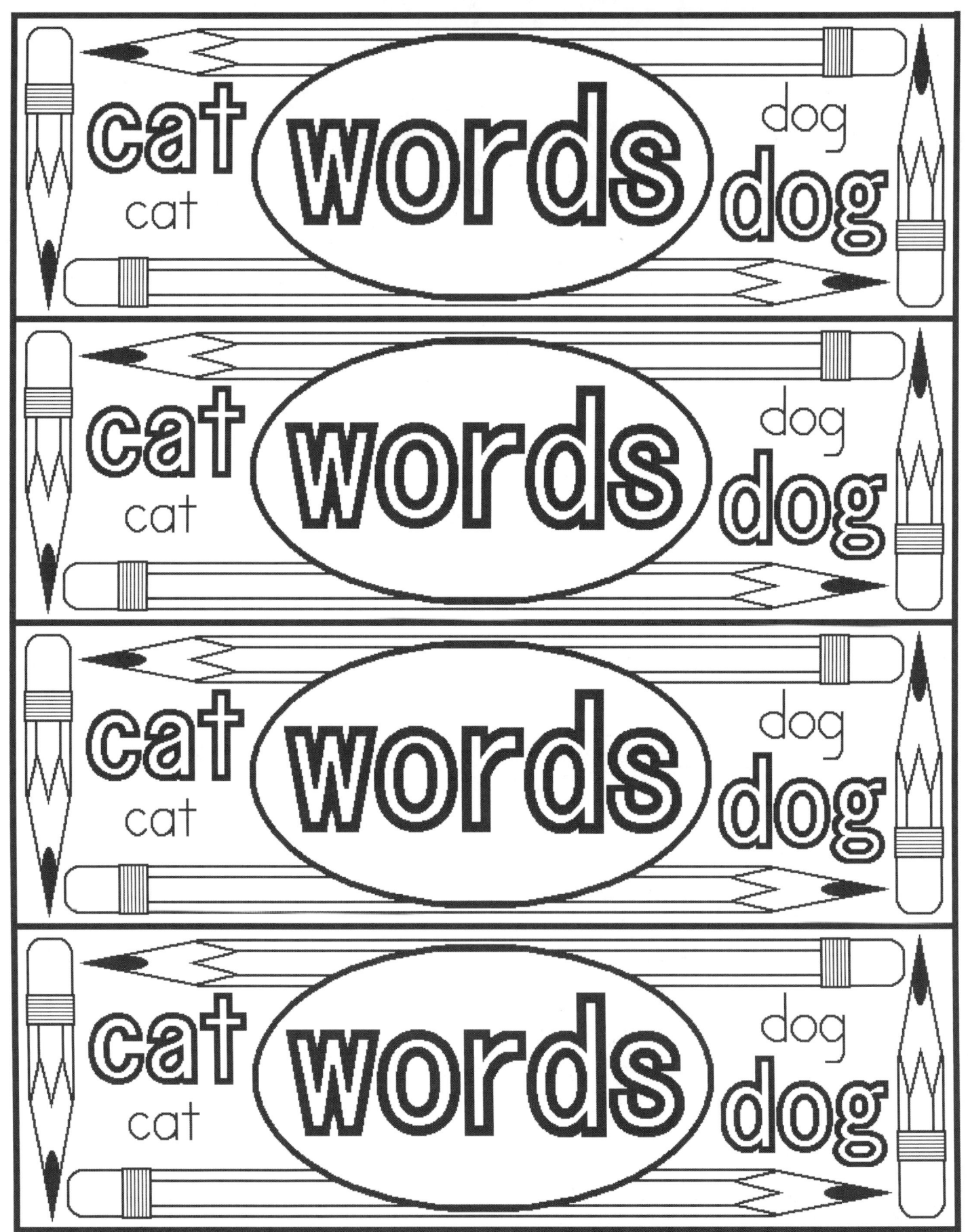

cat cat **words** dog dog

cat cat **words** dog dog

cat cat **words** dog dog

cat cat **words** dog dog

www.MisterKindergarten.com ©2015 Dwayne Douglas Kohn

SIGHT WORD BRACELETS

would

would

would

would

www.MisterKindergarten.com ©2015 Dwayne Douglas Kohn

SIGHT WORD BRACELETS

you

you

you

you

www.MisterKindergarten.com ©2015 Dwayne Douglas Kohn

SIGHT WORD BRACELETS

your

your

your

your

www.MisterKindergarten.com ©2015 Dwayne Douglas Kohn

Made in the USA
Columbia, SC
22 August 2022